embellished

PLAGUE

Isha Mahmood

ISBN-13: 978-1548686123

In the Name of Allāh, the Most Gracious, the Most Merciful

to every girl that lives within you

and

to all the girls you've had to drown

if life was merciful enough, I would take you in my arms and sing you a lullaby so sweet.

you are so much

so much

so let me evoke your existence,

let me bring you back to life one last time,

I promise to put you back to sleep,

when everything is over.

Contents

TEDDY BEARS AND SHATTERED DREAMS

"Do it for the children."

"They don't deserve to be miserable."

let's hate each other for the rest of our lives

damage each other for the rest of our lives

and,

be good parents to our children.

soaked eyes and wet pillows

smiling teddy bears

and stars above my bead

smashing and clattering sounds

shouting and pushing

cursing and crying

her small hands covering her ears

pinched eyes

go to sleep

go to sleep

It's okay teddy bears. Everything is fine.

a blank paper

colored crayons

she paints with the colors of blue

"What are you painting sweetheart?"

the teacher asks.

she longed for them to love one another

maybe then she would believe it

when they said

"We love you so much"

how could she possibly understand

the belonging beauty in something so ugly

all she could see

was the pain she was causing her mother

for being her child

she felt like an embellished plague

sitting in her beautifully decorated room

soaking up the words of her father,

that made her mother cry on her fragile shoulders

"If it wasn't for the children, I would've left you long ago."

if they belittle your sorrow

be brave enough to create

something so beautiful,

so beautiful out of it

be brave enough to see,

the beauty of what it has created within you

the tables will turn

your pain will become your victim

the day her heart was torn apart

was the day art was born

and it is both a blessing and a curse

it beautifies your hurting

freezes your healing

it is both your escape

and your prison

lights switched off

a dark room

her mind wide awake, creating scenarios from the noise

she learned to comfort the living and the dead

grabbing all her teddy bears

she was trying to console the lifeless

I guess,

she was trying to console herself

and her mother,

her mother became her child

"don't worry mother. I am you little mom now."

all the hurt

all the letdown

made her cherish the smallest things

she saw beauty

and love

in the most odd places

and she was happy with that

she was happy because,

she knew

as long as she could love

she could survive

for most, she was bizarre

she was too much of an adult

too much of a child,

both at the very same time

and she could simply not understand why

why she was different

I guess

she was busy being a grown up

too occupied protecting her teddy bears from the hurt,

she wanted to prevent within herself

drying the tears of her mother

putting a smile on her face

after every slander

and although she tried to be happy

she was exhausted

her world lied within her parents

and her world was being torn apart

by the very people

she thought were her heroes

she had everything she could wish for

and a dress in every color

they made sure to adorn every materialistic aspect of
her life

but she felt like a burden

because the very daughter

they were spoiling so much

in the name of love

was the cause to their misery

WOUNDED

we are all

works of art

in desperate need of interpretation by others

I carry the paintbrush to my own canvas

and yet,

I long for others to complete my painting

In the garden of my heart

some flowers have corroded and died

some I did not take care of

some did not take care of me

so corrupt me with your aptitude

for you possess the most beautiful fragrance

so conceive me,

shape me, like you

and then

we shall feed off

of each others awakening

and then

when we have managed to feed off of each other

when we've read each other

to the extent

that we've sucked the souls out of our bodies

you will slowly corrode again,

Your beautiful fragrance will turn into a distasteful
odor

my face will grow older and cold,

my soul will be tired

and you will remain like the many others,

a dead flower in the garden of my heart

sometimes

those who claim to love you

are the ones to put all their energy into changing you

they will try to recreate your shades

to their liking

do not change

do not change

leave small clues and traces

in the places where your heart belongs

and a soul like yours

will recognize you

recognize your art

It is ironic

how we seek love

in *people*

we search so desperately for it

we fear that it doesn't exist

and we forget

oh, how we forget

that love lies within us

and when it lies within you

it is to be seen everywhere

and

as long as you can find love

within yourself

you **are** the love you seek

Love. We speak so highly of you. Pretending to understand what you are.

We embellish you with superficial explanations, love is this, and love is that. Why do we tend to seek you in everyone but ourselves?

Love. We speak so highly of you, we end up belittling you.

We've turned love into a trade. You give, and you take.

Love, we've torn you apart, mocked love in the name of love.

We tend to accept the love we think we deserve, we narrow love to our own persona.

We believe love to be everything that they do and what we see, everything they say and what we hear.

But love lies in everything they do and what we don't see, everything they think and what we don't hear.

Love is so much more than what we make it out to be, and it is less than what we want it to be.

The love we dream of so desperately is not to be found in this world.

And the love we do have, we don't cherish

People will expect you to stop loving a person you once loved, only because they did you wrong.

It's not your fault,

that their love wasn't sincere. Your love was real, and you can't help that in a million years.

If you love, you love with all your heart and even if a decade passed, you'd still remember all the good things, because that's what matters. You remember **your** love for them, instead of **their** wrongdoings.

As long as you knew your love was sincere. You've done everything you could possibly do, to save something that wasn't ever yours to begin with.

And it's beautiful to try, and fail trying.

it is so beautiful

so beautiful

to give love

in return of hate

it is the most liberating feeling

to stay beautiful

after going through a pile of ugliness

It is when he said

''you haven't done anything to prove your love.''

she stepped away

and left

it is possible that your hurting seemed too beautiful

too appreciated and loved by the very you

you just learned to spread your wings

and love the failure,

embrace the past

and it is when people see you so comfortable in your aching

they take the dagger of jealousy

and stab you

and it is ironic

that they aim at past sorrows

but instead they create completely new

and fresh wounds

for you to heal

all over again

I've found that art

does not come from happiness

I meet happiness

I prefer loneliness

I find contentment unpleasant

I write

I write

I write

about the heartaches of life

I search for the pain that has no name

the monotony of happiness

creates an emptiness inside of me

so I search for the pain

that has no name

I have seen

what was in between

two lovers

and their dreams

I have heard

screams of the innocent

laughs of the devil

he laughed

she screamed

she cried

while all he could ever do,

was feed his ego and his pride

a dozen of lies

tears shed in despise

now when I look into my eyes

I see the poison you fed me with

these eyes turned red

you won

your poison led to my death

the walls whispered my name

oh love, what a shame

you don't even recognize the places

from where you came

and he continued to cut me open

and sprinkle salt upon my wounds

and smirk,

thinking I didn't see

It seemed as if he was embracing himself

through me

and I was just a passage

for him to welcome his true devilry

and why wouldn't he?

I had seen such little love

that in everything I did seek

even a madman's 'love' for me,

would seem like,

true bliss

I could visualize myself to you on a piece of paper. I could write you my whole mind. I could spend hours in the attempt of re-creating myself to you, and I know it's wrong. It's so wrong, that whenever you look at me with confusion in your eyes and tension in your voice for not truly understanding me, I become upset. And so I try, I try to change and make it easier for you to see me. I want you to see me. I am un-puzzling myself and removing parts of me, only to be envisioned by you. But then in the end, how much of me is left for you to understand? how much of me are you going to appreciate? I will be left with an incomplete me, and I will forever regret that I with such sanguinity thought, that you could bring out something better. I am a deception. An illusion, non-existent. A doll, a puppet. Your vision. Who am I? I carry the paintbrush to my canvas. My canvas is my body, my mind. I handed the brush to you and now you're not giving it back. I wanted you to solve the puzzle in me, but with my own very hands I've burned all the pieces and I don't know if I will ever find myself again.

she sat down and wondered if peace would ever come her way

she wondered, oh she wondered

will she then be recovered?

she then glanced at the auburn autumn leaves

they were once alive

now they are in grief

but they are yet to rise

by and by

how beautiful is suffering

she thought to herself

one must die, to rise above

one must fall, to be renewed

it's the circle

it's eternal

and in the memory

of who we used to be

I choose to cherish our love

Forever

have you ever been under water for longer than you should?

I hear myself loud and clear

I wish I could stay under here forever

all I hear is me

there's no you, no them

no one to find faults in me

I feel so free

It's so sad

how you envied me

you tried to aim at me

with your words of hurt and misery

but now you will see me rise from my absence

and you will witness it while it happens

oh, how bizarre

your face suddenly saddens

you aimed in the wrong directions

my 'imperfections' and personal tensions?

you have taught me

not to fear the fearsome, and isn't it ironic,

you fear me

you fear me for a reason.

I am everything you are too proud, to fear.

it took her so long

to find worth within herself

and she is still struggling

because she grew up in a home

where her feelings were overlooked

and her opinions were belittled

so how could she possibly believe,

that she meant something to anyone

and when people told her

know your worth

she did not know how to determine her worth

and so,

she let the people around her decide her worth

so when they treated her like they did

she thought nothing of it,

because for her

it felt natural

to feel like a pigeon

she knew how it felt

to be neglected,

to go unnoticed

this made her heart so tender

if a person said something in a conversation of many

and went unnoticed,

she would turn to that person immediately

look them in the eye

and insist

that they tell her what they were about to say

without hesitation

for she found,

that whenever she saw people happy

it fulfilled her

and if she saw someone sad,

she would be sad

and feel helpless

It's okay to feel beautiful, and I mean, not physically. Physical beauty doesn't matter, and it is more of a curse than a blessing. It's okay to feel like a beautiful person, and be proud of the heart that you have.

So many people overlook the importance of a beautiful and giving heart. It's so normal of people to appreciate physical beauty over the beauty of the soul, and therefore, to everyone that carries a beautiful heart. A beautiful scarred heart to be more specific. Know that you're so special.

Being kind, loving and tender after going through ugliness is the biggest blessing. You are precious for not letting the actions of others have an impact on your personality.

We lack beautiful people. We lack beautiful hearts.

Every human being on this earth **will** suffer from pain, one way or another. As human beings, it's impossible to outrun something like hurt and pain.

But to stay beautiful is so special, so unique.

It's common to hear, that people become coldhearted.

But to not let anyone dim your light is the biggest gift you can ever give yourself.

And people will tell you, that you're weak for being kind and giving.

No, you're the strongest person in this whole wide world.

You're a gift to every person around you.

Don't ever think of love as a trade. It's with the mentality of giving and taking in love, that you'll experience hurt and disappointment. Don't try to find love in others, because you *are* the love you seek.

If you will, you can possess the most powerful love and you'll leave people in awe of it. And isn't that the most beautiful thing?

And even if people don't seem to understand you, don't be disheartened.

People who constantly seek the proof of your love will never understand it, and they will only pay attention to the materialistic things you do for them.

Always remember,

You are not for everyone, and everyone is certainly not for you.

I tried, so much

to show you all of me

I read out my poems to you

and I expected you

to look me in the eyes

and recognize

all the galaxies I behold

in my mind

and I looked at you

with such longing,

that you would see me

for me

but,

in a blink of an eye

you devalued my very existence

I felt so small

when I heard you say

pretty girls cannot be intelligent, and intelligent girls
cannot be pretty.

after a very long time

I have realized

that I

should never have given anyone

the power,

to make me

excuse my character

my way of thinking

I have wasted too much of me

to untangle myself to you

and get knocked down

in the process

after many efforts

I have realized

that I am simply not for everyone,

and everyone is simply not for me.

and it all boils down to the fact

that you need love

and that *love* is to be found within yourself

you are capable of so much,

you are capable of self-creation,

and

self-destruction

so, love every thing about you

and be shameless about it,

the moment you doubt yourself

is the moment you allow yourself to be vulnerable

you start believing that you need people

to love you, in order to feel loved

when really, you need to love yourself

in order to feel loved

no one can make you genuinely happy in life,

if you think that the only source to happiness and love
is in everything,

but yourself.

GOD'S LOVE

Verily, in the remembrance of Allah do hearts find rest (13:28)

she longs
for her head to hit the ground in Sujood
because
that is truly the only time
she feels the presence of Perfection
in an imperfect world

the world
labels me
as such and such
I am belittled
and pitied
for being a woman

but
You wash away
all the stamps from my body, O Allah
the stamps that your creations have given me
your creations embellish me
then call me a plague

but
You
You
take off of me
every accusation
every delusional embellishment

and You love me

O, Allah
You love me
for the woman I am

while the creations love me
only if I am the woman
they want me to be

and she was in awe
of His love
whenever she laid on the prayer mat
and closed her eyes
she felt at peace
for in that moment
she felt like
she was in the hands of God
and no harm
no sorrow
could come her way
and she could feel the Presence of Him
so Powerful
so Beautiful
so Merciful

it was when God answered
a prayer of mine
which I had forgotten all about
that I poured my heart out to Him
and asked for forgiveness
for my selfishness
and thanked Him
for loving me
despite it

God loves us so much
He remembers our dreams
even the ones we forget
and God hears our prayers
the ones we have suppressed
deep down in our hearts
we don't even hear them ourselves,
but He does
and He knows everything about us
isn't it beautiful
we struggle
to explain people
what we feel
we have difficulty
in wording it
but to God
we don't have to utter a word
for He knows

Often times, as young children we are taught about the punishment and anger of Allah, before the love and mercy of Allah. I have seen mothers telling their children, "Allah will punish you if you don't eat with your right hand."

Or make up things like, "it's haram to eat a lot of candy. Allah gets angry at children who eat too much candy"

A 7-8 year old child will not learn to love their Creator growing up, if they're constantly being scared to death, thinking about Allah as a brutal punisher. How will a child find Allah to be merciful in that age? A child is not capable of seeing the bigger picture, the only thing they'll understand is that Allah punishes children for eating candy and eating with their left hand.

Anyone who does not show mercy to our children nor acknowledge the right of our old people is not one of us – Prophet Muhammad (Peace be upon him)

Some children grow up in a violent household, they face violence in the name of Islam. Some parents don't think about the greater harm they're causing. They may think that they're doing good and disciplining their children with violence, but they don't think about the consequences afterwards.

Later on in life they complain about their children being disobedient, or just overall hateful towards Islam.

Allah is the Most Merciful. Islam does not promote violence in any way. It's the most peaceful religion, and whoever thinks otherwise doesn't know anything about Islam.

Unfortunately a lot of children grow up fearing Allah, before they learn to love Allah, when in fact, with children you need to be tender and kind, you have to teach them how *easy* it is to love Allah.

Even as youngsters it can be quite difficult to view Allah as The Most Merciful, Most Forgiving, especially if you don't do your own research before listening to other's interpretation of the religion. A lot of religious preachers tend to sound aggressive, harsh and judging in their tone when giving Da'wah (Translated to 'Invitation', means preaching of Islam), which makes younger people break away from Islam, or feel worthless in the eyes of Allah.

"O Messenger of Allah! It is a great Mercy of God that you are gentle and kind towards them; for, had you been harsh and hard-hearted, they would all have broken away from you" (Quran 3:159)

Prophet Muhammad (Peace be upon him) was soft spoken, and kind hearted, and was not judgmental.

Make 70 excuses for your believing brother and sister before you judge them –
Imam Ali (AS)

How many excuses do we make for our fellow Muslims before judging them? Not even one.

Allah said*: "O you who have believed, avoid much [negative] assumption. Indeed, some assumption is sin. And do not spy or backbite each other. Would one of you like to eat the flesh of his brother when dead? You would detest it. And fear Allah; indeed, Allah is Accepting of repentance and Merciful." [49:12]*

This verse indicates that Allah is The Accepting of Repentance and The Merciful. Allah may have forgiven the sins of the person you're still backbiting and judging, and this is where the problem lies.
It seems as if some people like to take the role of God.

Prophet Muhammad (Peace be upon him) said:
"(…) I swear by Allah – there is no God but He – one of you may perform the deeds of the people of Paradise till there is naught but an arm's length between him and it, when that which has been written will outstrip him so that he performs the deeds of the people of the Hell Fire – one of you may perform the deeds of the people of the Hell Fire, till there is naught but an arm's length between him and it, when that

which has been written will overtake him so that he performs the deeds of the people of Paradise and enters therein.''

You may see someone who's not acting in accordance to Islam, and judge him or her for being a 'bad' Muslim, or a bad person but only Allah knows the Niyyah (intention) of that person.

Imam Jafar as-Sadiq said:
''If you see something you don't like in a brother, try to find 1-70 excuses for him, and if you can't find an excuse say 'There might be an excuse, but I don't know it.' ''

Emphasising these matters is important, because unfortunately the only people who tend to push Muslims further away from Islam are Muslims.

Your Imaan (faith, belief) can be the highest, but that doesn't change that you're a human and you have feelings.
If you tell an intelligent person that they're stupid over a hundred times, that person will begin to doubt their intelligence.
If you tell a beautiful (physically beautiful) person, that they're ugly over a hundred times, that person will doubt their beauty.
In the same way, if you tell a Muslim person that they're not Muslim, they're a Kaafir (disbeliever), or they'll go to hell, it is only normal for that person to

doubt their own Imaan, and question himself or herself for even being a Muslim.

Prophet Muhammad (peace be upon him) said:

"If a man addresses his brother as, 'O' Disbeliever' (Kaafir) it returns to one of them; either it is as he said or it returns to him."

Being born a Muslim doesn't necessarily mean you have more knowledge of Islam than others.
It can be quite the opposite actually.
Sometimes you have to find Allah yourself, and the journey is quite difficult at first, but when you finally find Allah, everything in life will become easy for you.
As a young Muslim woman I found it quite hard to take refuge in Allah because of the way the Muslim community tend to portray religion,
but when I finally did, it was like getting everything I had ever needed back to me.

I say
I am in love
with my Creator
I adore my Creator
and when I think of His love for me
I feel ashamed
and angry at myself
for not appreciating His love
as much as I should
I realize being a human
follows being ungrateful
and I wish my love was perfect
but Perfection
is only exclusive to Allah

I was becoming cold
indifferent
and sad
and Allah
took all the sadness out of me
like it was never there
and I faced difficulties
with faith
that Allah is with me
in my downfall
and rise
and He will love me
even after thousands of failures
and thousands of sins
It will never be late
to turn to Him

In prayer
I could sit for hours
without uttering a word
only tears
falling down my cheeks
and my conversation with Allah
would not have to be an exchange of words
all it would be
was
a feeling
a Presence
that would make everything
feel like nothing
I would be so vulnerable
and yet so strong
for I know that
I am not alone

I, THE WOMAN

In the body
you call fragile
feminine
frail,
and soft
lies a warrior
runs blood
as hot as fire

if you love me
my skin will feel
like the softest flower,
but
demean me
and my skin will feel as rough
as a stone
I am a woman

in my fragile body
lies everything
you love and hate

let me remind you
in case you have forgotten
my beauty does not revolve around my appearance
this is not my skill
for which you believe I am fulfilled
define me perfect
and I will tell you
your world is delusionary
and incorrect
I don't compare myself to the weaker interpretation
this society has given my race
it is rather
the places that I embrace
the intelligence I behold
the mazes I have solved
the staircases I have walked
they are the true me
they define who I am
and who I aim to be
don't mistake me for another face of eye-candy
I am a maze
few keep up
most lose and go astray

I am from another universe
I wander here
I uncover here
the mysteries of the soul I behold
I don't claim to know myself
I don't
I am not in control
I do not settle
for the materialistics and decor
so they ask me
what do you want more
what do you want more
I am not from this universe
what I miss
what I reminisce
is a bliss
that is beyond
the understanding
of this world

I wish they could see
past the structure of my face
shape of my eyes and brows
size of my lips and nose
the physical beauty I behold
is nothing more than an illusion
it's a delusion
many people
fail and fall
they think so small, so small
don't love me for my appearance
tell me what you genuinely feel
and in an instance
I shall praise you
for your understanding heart
for you have felt my presence
in your heart and soul
for me,
that's power
beyond physical beauty
that is
what makes me whole

a girl was taught by the whole world around her,
to hate herself
for being brown
they praise Allah
for being the Creator of beauty
and at the very same time
they shame the creation of Allah
for being created in golden brown skin
no one stopped me
when I with such sanguinity
applied 'fair and lovely'
on my face
a hope
was what that little girl saw
in the eyes of her mother
who too
was mocked for the colour of her skin
that maybe her daughter will become 'fair and lovely'
she'll be fair
and loved for it

they say

if you behold physical beauty
you simply cannot be intelligent

and if you are intelligent
you simply cannot behold physical beauty

physical beauty
is a curse
you will aim towards the hearts of people
your whole life
and miss
every single time

a woman
is so powerful
she is
if she wills
the most intimidating creature
walking on earth
and that is why
the world
hates her so much
they cut her wings
and
tarnish
the beauty of her being
because
they fear
everything
she is capable of becoming

even today
in my culture
my women are silenced
they are muted
they are taught to 'adjust'
tumhari zabaan kenchi ki tarha tez hai
(your tongue is as sharp as a knife)
my zabaan
is my weapon
do not, threaten
my right to speak
do not educate me
to then suffocate me ever so brutally
do not educate me,
I repeat
and then hand me to a grown boy
who still needs his mother
to wash his dirty clothes
my tongue
speaks my knowledge
I stand here
hand in hand with my independence
you say,
my zabaan speaks my ignorance
no
it is my strength
my bravery
in my culture
your moral rights are not rightfully given to you,
sometimes,

you have to steal your own rights
and I will fight
do not take advantage of my unworldliness

I am so much
and so little
at the very same time
you love me
and despise me
I am either your treasure
or a disgrace to woman nature
I am tangled in between
the blame
and guilt
of being a human
I am so much
so valuable
carrying the sins
and honour
of numerous people
I am so little
so worthless
carrying so many people
have suppressed my existence
dimmed my light
I walk around
described as
ghar ki raunak
the joy of the home
whilst all I am
is an embellished plague

before I am a human
I am a worry
I carry the burden of honour
on my shoulders
and it is my,
and my responsibility only
to protect
and preserve it
and maybe that is why
they rush
to marry me off

"She is your responsibility now."

"Anything she does will be on you."

it is
the woman
who gives birth to the man
and still
it is the man
who destroys
and claims
their rights
upon
women
it is as if
we, women
carry venom
in our wombs
and
we spread
the disease
of misogyny
as soon
as we allow
our sons
and husbands
to demean the role
of the women
in their lives

God is not in need
of any reason
to love me
He loves
my naked soul
my naked mind
and yet the creation
craves so much of me
in order
to be able
to love me

and you need to know
that you are of so much worth
even when the world
strips
every label of honour
off of you
you are of so much worth
because their labels on you
are made
for their own benefit
they were never for you
in fact
they were bad for you
they held you down
so be happy
when you are told
by the ignorant
that you are of no worth
for that means
that the bird
is miraculously
growing out her cut wings
she is
being set free
by herself

"A woman's rights? What does she need them for."

"Islam has already given her all her rights."

"Stupid feminists."

Allah, The Creator
has given me all my rights
but you refuse,
as the creation
to enforce those rights?

because of your ingrained misogyny,
that runs so deeply
in the veins
of your beloved culture,
you are too afraid
to open the Holy Book of Allah
and acknowledge my rights

when your son keeps your honour
you love him
when your son does not keep your honour
you love him

when your daughter keeps your honour
you love her
when your daughter does not keep your honour
you hate her

the saddest part is
that you've been taught
to hate the woman you are
how haven't you been taught,
that
the biggest blessing
is to be a woman

and the most liberating feeling
is to know
that even though the creation
has made ugly
my womanhood
Allah, The Exalted, The Most Powerful
beautifies me

they say
we appreciate strong women
we are inspired by strong women
they say
we need more strong women
as long as
they are not
from our household

why is it
that when people
discuss,
and spend hours to literally excuse
why a woman deserves respect
they conclude
that it's because, she's a daughter, a sister, a wife
no
no
no
I deserve
and I am worthy of respect
regardless of being
attached
to these labels,
which without
you have chosen to give me no value

you kill the woman I have the potential to be
and you give birth
to a woman
who's not really me

my fragrance can reach heights
no one has ever had the imagination
to dream of

and I guess
that's what scares you the most

women
bend over for the men in their lives,
out of fear
and
men think
it's out of respect and admiration

why are some men so obsessed with claiming the role
of God?

you cannot
diminish
the life of a discriminated woman
just because you don't live her life

so when you say
"she's lying,"
"it can't be possible."

you belittle her scars
you demean her very existence

she studied hard
and chose
the highest
most praiseworthy
education
she was known as a 'good girl'
she did everything
to not tarnish the 'honour' of her family
the very 'honour'
her brothers
had tarnished again and again

and still,
when she walked amongst the people from her culture
she'd feel apologetic
for not being a boy

societal norms are not religious doctrine.

if you wish
to find me,
the woman
in societal norms

you will never find me
because,
the woman I truly am
is too powerful
to walk
in chains

how I wish
you wouldn't struggle
to love me
how I wish
you would stop
shaming my womanhood
if just
you could look me in the eyes
and say
"I am proud of you."
everything would be different.

I've disappointed myself
numerous times
by asking myself
if I am truly a disappointment?

no.

the moment I allow myself to believe that,
is the moment I allow myself to be my own prisoner.

my existence belongs to God.
God will never hate me,
nor be disappointed in me.

God is greater than everyone, so who are these people
for which I'm questioning myself?

the bitter truth of a misogynistic man's life
is the fact that
he needs a woman

you cut off the wings of a bird, because you're afraid it might fly.

honour based abuse exists, whether you acknowledge it or not.

Isn't it ironic? How we perceive women to be weak, because of their loving hearts, their easily flowing tears, their forgiving nature.

And men? Men are strong, they're not weak and if they are, they're like women. Which is bad, apparently.

Because being a woman is a sign of weakness.

Real strength lies in your mercy, forgiveness, softness and love.

Not in the strength of your fists.

The beloved Prophet (Peace and Blessings of Allah be upon him) said:

"When a boy is born, then he brings one Noor (light) and when a girl is born, then she brings two Noors."

"If parents are kind and generous towards their daughters, then they will be so close to Him (The Holy Prophet Peace and Blessings of Allah be Upon Him) in Jannah, like one finger is to the next."

"The person who is faced with hardship due to his daughters, and makes Sabr (is patient), then his daughters will be a Pardah (curtain) between him and the Hell-fire."

The next few pages are from a **stepfeed** article, written by Law student Rayana Khalaf.

1. Islam gave women their basic rights centuries before the West did

"Women in 7th century Arabia had rights not extended to most women in the West till recent centuries over 1,000 years later," writes Huffington Post's Jim Garrison.

Women in pre-Islamic Arabia were reportedly barred from basic human and civil rights. They were considered inferior to men, and therefore treated as property. Women had very little control over their marriages and could not inherit property.

When Islam was introduced in the sixth century, women's status improved substantially.

Islamic law made the education of girls a sacred duty and gave women the right to own and inherit property. Islam also imposed women's consent as a condition for legitimate marriage contracts.

Islam was actually the first religion to give women rights of inheritance.

Meanwhile, women in America and Europe were denied the right to own and manage property until the 18th century.

2. Islam tackled female infanticide

In the pre-Islam pagan society, it was the custom to bury alive unwanted female newborns. Islam put an end to the barbaric practice and forbade it. Plus, it **condemns** parents who are disappointed with the birth of female newborns, which is unfortunately still a common attitude in current Muslim and Arab societies.

3. The Quran encourages women to learn and work

Muslims believe that the first verses revealed to Prophet Muhammed were the first five verses in Surat Al-Alaq ("The Clot"), which orders people to seek knowledge.

Seeking knowledge is thus obligatory for every Muslim, male and female.

"It is the duty of every Muslim man and woman to seek knowledge," the prophet is quoted as saying.

It seems only fitting then that the University of Al Qarawiyyin in Morocco, the world's oldest-standing universities, which has the world's oldest library, was founded by a Muslim woman in the 850s.

The Quran also encourages women to work and earn money by entitling them to fair pay.

"...And their Lord responded to them, 'Never will I allow to be lost the work of [any] worker among you, whether male or female; you are of one another'." [Quran 3:195]

4. "For his day, the Prophet Muhammad was a feminist"

"For his day, the Prophet Muhammad was a feminist," writes Lisa Beyer in an article for Time magazine. By laying down the Islamic doctrine that dictates women's rights, the prophet was arguably the first feminist in history.

Countering the widespread exploitation of women, he ordered men to honor and respect them.

In one of his last commands before his death, he kept repeating, "I command you to be kind and considerate to women." In another hadith, he said, "It is only the generous in character who is good to women, and only the evil one who insults them."

He also frowned upon fathers who insult their daughters and favor their sons over them, saying the birth of a girl is a "blessing".

Known for treating them kindly and helping with house work, the prophet led by example in his relationships with his wives, many of whom were working women.

He even decreed that women have a right to sexual satisfaction.

5. Men and women are equal in Islamic duties

There is no denying that Islam asserts gender roles by portraying men as providers and "maintainers of women". But, when it comes to the fundamental pillars of Islam and spiritual duties and promised rewards, men and women are seen as equals.

Islamic law generally does not discriminate between genders in the regulations pertaining to prayer, fasting, charity, pilgrimage, doing good deeds... It also promises all Muslims, men and women, similar rewards and punishments.

"Whose acts righteously, whether male or female and is a believer, we will surely grant him a pure life; and We will surely bestow on such their reward according to the best of their work." [Quran 16:9]

6. The Quran describes marriage as companionship

Several excerpts from the Quran describe the relationship between a man and his wife as one between partners and companions, refuting the misconception that Muslim women are their husbands' servants.

Muslim men are obliged to respect their wives and treat them with kindness no matter the circumstances.

"Live with them (your wives) in kindness. For if you dislike them - perhaps you dislike a thing and Allah makes therein much good." [Quran 4:19]

"And of His signs is that He created for you from yourselves mates that you may find tranquillity in them; and He placed between you affection and mercy. Indeed in that are signs for a people who give thought." [Quran 30:21]

7. Having multiple wives was first allowed for the sake of women

Islam first allowed polygamy for the sake of widows and orphans who have no means of survival.

The only Quranic verse that speaks about polygamy is believed to have been revealed after the Battle of Uhud, which led to the death of many Muslim men who left behind families in need of support.

Islamic law allows men, unlike their female counterparts, to be wed to four spouses at a time. But, not so fast. People often forget that this is only permissible within a tight frame of conditions.

The Quran clearly states that men can marry more than one woman if and only if he treats them fairly. "But if you fear that you will not be just, then [marry only] one," Surat An-Nisaa ("The Women") states.

But, the surah then decrees, "You will never be able to be equal between wives, even if you should strive to do so". This makes Islam-approved polygamy near impossible to attain.

8. Muslim women have the right to divorce

In Islam, marriage is seen as a mutually-beneficial contract, in which a man and a woman agree to the terms of the marriage.

While traditions do not endorse this practice, Muslim couples are free to sign a pre-nuptial agreement. In the agreement, a woman can dictate any terms and conditions she wishes for, just like in civil marriages.

She can set the amount of money she would receive in the event of a divorce, the right to continue her education, the right to be the only wife...

She can also stipulate the right to ask for a divorce herself because otherwise, a divorce generally cannot be completed without the husband's approval.

So, how did the status of women in the Muslim world spiral downhill?

Fundamentalist interpretations of Quranic verses, which are sometimes taken out of context, as well as long-standing patriarchal, lie in the heart of the problem.

The Quran can be seen distributing gender roles by depicting men as providers of the household and women as caregivers - as that was the social paradigm when the holy book was revealed. This is mainly the reason behind the apparent discrimination between genders, when it comes to matters of inheritance, for instance.

That distribution of gender roles has been exploited. Many men have hand-picked Islamic teachings and used them to assert their dominance over women, interpreting the Quran according to their own patriarchal interests. (Muslim scholars are mostly male - surprise, surprise.)

Meanwhile, crucial Islamic teachings, such as "There is no compulsion in religion" and the laws pertaining to women's rights, are often disregarded.

Plus, over the years, the line separating religion from customs and traditions has been blurred, as societal norms are often mistaken for religious doctrine.

So, before bashing Islam for oppressing women, make sure to distinguish Islamic principles from norms and common practice.

source: http://stepfeed.com/this-is-how-islam-led-the-world-with-women-s-rights-0090

Article written by Rayana Khalaf.

LETTERS TO MY FUTURE DAUGHTER

The day you arrive will be the best day of my life.
The day you arrive, is the day I'll know that God has blessed me, with the most beautiful gift ever.

A daughter.

And one can just begin to try and tarnish the beauty of your being.
One can just try.

"My daughter is equal to a son."

No.

You, my baby girl.
You, are beyond everything I will ever get in a son.

I will never allow you
to feel guilty for being a girl.
I will never allow you,
to demean yourself because of your gender.

Remember,
Please. Remember.

These people will never understand the beauty of your
being,
but you. You must always remember,
you are everything.
Everything, these people say you can't be.

my love
my love
they say that a man will give you protection,
because of his harsh nature and robust body
he will make you feel safe
because he is 'strong'
.. a man,
a man is your guardian

but believe me when I tell you
no man will ever make me feel as safe,
and as protected
as I will feel when I hold you in my arms for the first
time

because in that very moment,
when I hold you for the first time,
a force, stronger than anything I've ever felt will strike
me.

Motherhood.

My dear love,
I will forgive every 'mistake' of yours,
and I will forget without hesitation..
but if there comes a day you decide,
that your physical appearance defines you,

I will have a hard time forgetting..

Before becoming a pretty face.
Become **you**.

I promise,
I will do everything in my power,
to make you smile from the bottom of your heart.
I will do anything to not let happiness and contentment
become a delusion.

My love,
the whole world might turn cold and cruel,
and kindness might just become a myth,
but,
never let this world dim your light,
you have so much of it
you can light up everyone,
and put a smile, even on the most dimmest of people.

My dear love,
it is not bad
to compromise
and sacrifice
for the people you love, and for the people that love
you.
Be like a cloud
you're there and yet you're not
people will seek more of you
to get to hear your sweet laughter
and soft voice

but if these very same people demean you
and belittle your character
let them know
you'll turn into everything they never thought of you.
Sharp like a knife,
hot like lava,
they'll be afraid to seek more of you
they will not be able to look you in the eyes,
and that's when you know,
you have enough courage to teach those you love a
lesson,
for not appreciating you.

The future of our community is in our hands.
Let's raise our future children, to be everything our
elders didn't allow us to be in the name of culture.

My tulip…

When the whole world recognized me for nothing but my physical appearance. You saw me.
In an instant, you saw who I truly was.
The day I showed you my first piece of poetry, you were in awe and I saw true excitement in your eyes, I saw… well, I saw that you were proud. That feeling still wanders in my body and my mind. To know that my best friend was proud of me, to see the excitement and the appreciation in your eyes for who I truly am.
Not something I was quite used to.
No one ever made me believe in myself as much as you did, and you still do.
The more gratitude I show you, the less it seems.
We've been through everything bad and good, and you are truly the only person I know, who will love and cherish me forever. Even if we are miles away, I know deep down that you will love me and I will love you.
Because what we have is more than friendship, it's something completely different.
I believe that a soul mate doesn't have to be found in a romantic partner, and as cliché as it sounds, you are just that, and so much more.
When I first met you, I would never have thought that you'd be one of the most important people in my life.

Today, I can't imagine a life without you.
Thank you for always being my support system.

Thank you for always making me believe that I'm so much more.
Thank you for being in my life.

Until next time…

You can contact Isha Mahmood through her e-mail:
Isha.loona@wearemin.co

20833476R00074

Printed in Poland
by Amazon Fulfillment
Poland Sp. z o.o., Wrocław